# IT'S TIME TO LEARN ABOUT JESUS CHRIST

# It's Time to Learn about Jesus Christ

## Walter the Educator

**SKB**

Silent King Books
A WhichHead Entertainment Imprint

First Printing, 2024

## Disclaimer

It's Time to Learn about Jesus Christ is a collectible little learning book by Walter the Educator that belongs to the Little Learning Books Series. Collect them all and more books at WaltertheEducator.com

# JESUS CHRIST

# INTRO

Jesus Christ is one of the most influential figures in human history, revered as the Lord and Savior in Christianity. His teachings, life, and sacrificial death form the cornerstone of Christian faith, influencing billions of people across different cultures and eras. This little book seeks to explore the messiah of Jesus Christ, his historical and theological significance, and his role as Savior and Redeemer. It will delve into his life, ministry, teachings, and the impact he has had on individuals and societies throughout history.

# The Historical Context of Jesus Christ

Jesus of Nazareth was born around 4 BCE in Bethlehem, a small town in Judea, under Roman rule. His birth is traditionally celebrated by Christians on December 25, known as Christmas. The historical context of his life is critical to understanding his mission and message.

He lived during a time of political turmoil and religious expectation among the Jewish people, who were anticipating the coming of a Messiah, a savior who would liberate them from Roman oppression and restore the kingdom of Israel.

It's Time to Learn about
# Jesus Christ

Jesus' life and ministry are documented in the New Testament of the Bible, particularly in the four Gospels: Matthew, Mark, Luke, and John. Although these texts were written decades after his death, they provide the most comprehensive account of his life. Jesus grew up in Nazareth, a small village in Galilee, and worked as a carpenter before beginning his public ministry around the age of 30.

## It's Time to Learn about
# Jesus Christ

## The Ministry of Jesus

Jesus' ministry began with his baptism by John the Baptist in the Jordan River, an event that marked the beginning of his public work and was accompanied by a divine affirmation of his sonship. He then spent 40 days in the wilderness, fasting and being tempted by Satan, before returning to Galilee to preach the Kingdom of God.

# It's Time to Learn about
# Jesus Christ

His message centered around repentance, love, and the coming of God's Kingdom. He performed numerous miracles, such as healing the sick, raising the dead, feeding thousands with a few loaves of bread and fish, and calming storms, which demonstrated his authority and compassion. These miracles, combined with his profound teachings, attracted large crowds and followers.

## It's Time to Learn about
# Jesus Christ

## The Teachings of Jesus

Jesus' teachings were revolutionary and often counter-cultural. He emphasized love for God and neighbor as the greatest commandments, encapsulated in the well-known "Golden Rule": "Do unto others as you would have them do unto you" (Matthew 7:12).

# It's Time to Learn about
# Jesus Christ

His teachings were often conveyed through parables, which are simple stories with deep spiritual meaning that illustrate the values of the Kingdom of God, such as forgiveness, humility, and the love of God.

# It's Time to Learn about

# Jesus Christ

One of the most famous collections of his teachings is the Sermon on the Mount (Matthew 5-7), where he expounded on various aspects of righteous living, including the Beatitudes, which describe the blessings of those who embody virtues like meekness, mercy, and peacemaking. Jesus also challenged the religious leaders of his time, the Pharisees and Sadducees, accusing them of hypocrisy and legalism.

## It's Time to Learn about

# Jesus Christ

## The Identity of Jesus as the Messiah

A central question in Jesus' ministry was his identity as the Messiah. The term "Messiah" (Hebrew: Mashiach) means "anointed one" and refers to a deliverer promised in the Hebrew Scriptures. Many of Jesus' contemporaries expected a political and military leader who would overthrow Roman rule.

It's Time to Learn about
# Jesus Christ

However, Jesus redefined the concept of the Messiah as a spiritual Savior who would establish a heavenly, not earthly, kingdom.

It's Time to Learn about
# Jesus Christ

He identified himself as the Son of God, a claim that was both radical and controversial. In the Gospel of John, Jesus makes several "I am" statements (e.g., "I am the bread of life," "I am the light of the world," "I am the good shepherd") that reveal his divine nature and mission. His declaration, "Before Abraham was, I am" (John 8:58), directly alluded to God's name revealed to Moses in the burning bush (Exodus 3:14), implying his pre-existence and divinity.

## It's Time to Learn about
# Jesus Christ

**The Death and Resurrection of Jesus**

The climax of Jesus' life was his crucifixion and resurrection,
events that are central to Christian faith.

# It's Time to Learn about
# Jesus Christ

His death was the culmination of mounting opposition from the Jewish religious authorities, who accused him of blasphemy, and the Roman government, which saw him as a potential political threat.

## It's Time to Learn about
# Jesus Christ

Betrayed by one of his disciples, Judas Iscariot, Jesus was arrested, tried, and sentenced to death by crucifixion, which was a common Roman method of execution for criminals.

# It's Time to Learn about
# Jesus Christ

Christians believe that Jesus' death was not a tragic end, but a divine plan for the redemption of humanity.

# It's Time to Learn about
# Jesus Christ

According to Christian theology, humanity is separated from God due to sin, and Jesus' sacrificial death atoned for the sins of the world, offering salvation to all who believe in him.

## It's Time to Learn about
# Jesus Christ

This is encapsulated in the well-known verse, "For God so loved the world that he gave his one and only Son, that whoever believes in him shall not perish but have eternal life" (John 3:16).

# It's Time to Learn about

# Jesus Christ

Three days after his death, Jesus rose from the dead, an event known as the Resurrection. His resurrection is considered the cornerstone of Christian faith, as it demonstrates his victory over sin and death and affirms his divine nature.

# It's Time to Learn about
# Jesus Christ

The Apostle Paul wrote, "If Christ has not been raised, our preaching is useless and so is your faith" (1 Corinthians 15:14), emphasizing the importance of the resurrection to the Christian message.

## It's Time to Learn about
# Jesus Christ

### Jesus as the Savior

The concept of Jesus as Savior is rooted in his role in reconciling humanity with God. According to Christian belief, all people have sinned and fall short of the glory of God (Romans 3:23). Sin separates people from God, creating a spiritual chasm that cannot be bridged by human effort alone.

# It's Time to Learn about
# Jesus Christ

Jesus, as the sinless Son of God, willingly took upon himself the punishment for sin through his death on the cross, thereby satisfying the demands of justice and offering forgiveness and reconciliation to all who believe.

## It's Time to Learn about
# Jesus Christ

Jesus' role as Savior is also linked to the concept of grace. Grace is the unmerited favor of God, a gift that cannot be earned through good works or human effort.

## It's Time to Learn about
# Jesus Christ

Ephesians 2:8-9 states, "For it is by grace you have been saved, through faith, and this is not from yourselves; it is the gift of God, not by works, so that no one can boast."

# It's Time to Learn about
# Jesus Christ

This means that salvation is a gift from God, made possible through Jesus' sacrificial death and received through faith.

## It's Time to Learn about
# Jesus Christ

### The Impact of Jesus' Teachings

The teachings of Jesus have had a profound impact on individuals and societies throughout history. His message of love, forgiveness, and compassion has inspired countless acts of charity, social justice, and reconciliation.

## It's Time to Learn about
# Jesus Christ

Many hospitals, schools, and charitable organizations have been founded in his name, reflecting his call to care for the poor, sick, and marginalized.

# It's Time to Learn about
# Jesus Christ

Jesus' teachings have also shaped ethical and moral standards in many cultures. Concepts such as the inherent dignity of every person, the importance of forgiveness and reconciliation, and the value of humility and service are rooted in his teachings.

# It's Time to Learn about
# Jesus Christ

His example of sacrificial love has inspired movements for social change, including the abolition of slavery, the civil rights movement, and efforts to promote peace and reconciliation in conflict areas.

## It's Time to Learn about
# Jesus Christ

## The Spread of Christianity

After Jesus' resurrection, his disciples, who were eyewitnesses to these events, began to spread his message throughout the Roman Empire and beyond.

# It's Time to Learn about
# Jesus Christ

This movement, known as the early Christian church, faced significant opposition and persecution but continued to grow rapidly.

It's Time to Learn about
# Jesus Christ

The Apostle Paul, one of the most influential figures in early Christianity, played a key role in spreading the gospel to Gentile (non-Jewish) communities and establishing churches throughout Asia Minor, Greece, and Rome.

# It's Time to Learn about
# Jesus Christ

Christianity eventually became the dominant religion of the Roman Empire and spread throughout Europe, Asia, Africa, and the Americas. Today, Christianity is the world's largest religion, with over two billion followers from diverse cultural and ethnic backgrounds.

It's Time to Learn about

# Jesus Christ

### Personal Relationship with Jesus

Central to Christian faith is the belief that individuals can have a personal relationship with Jesus Christ. This relationship is not based on religious rituals or moral behavior but on faith in Jesus as Lord and Savior.

## It's Time to Learn about
# Jesus Christ

Through prayer, reading of Scripture, and the guidance of the Holy Spirit, Christians believe they can know Jesus personally and experience his presence and guidance in their lives.

# It's Time to Learn about
# Jesus Christ

This personal relationship transforms individuals, giving them a new identity as children of God and a sense of purpose and meaning. It also brings hope and assurance of eternal life. Jesus said, "I am the resurrection and the life. The one who believes in me will live, even though they die" (John 11:25), promising eternal life to those who trust in him.

# It's Time to Learn about
# Jesus Christ

### The Second Coming of Jesus

Christian eschatology, or the study of the end times, teaches that Jesus will return to earth in the future, a belief known as the Second Coming. This event is anticipated as the culmination of God's redemptive plan, where Jesus will judge the living and the dead and establish a new heaven and a new earth.

## It's Time to Learn about
# Jesus Christ

The exact timing of this event is unknown, but Christians are encouraged to live in a state of readiness, faithfully following Jesus and spreading his message of hope and salvation.

# It's Time to Learn about
# Jesus Christ

# OUTRO

Jesus Christ is not merely a historical figure but the Lord and Savior who offers hope, salvation, and a transformed life to all who believe in him.

His life, teachings, death, and resurrection have had an unparalleled impact on individuals and societies throughout history. His message of love, grace, and redemption continues to inspire and transform lives today.

**For those who seek to understand Jesus, the invitation remains open: "Come to me, all you who are weary and burdened, and I will give you rest" (Matthew 11:28). This is the essence of Jesus' message, an invitation to find peace, purpose, and eternal life in a personal relationship with him. Whether one approaches Jesus as a seeker, skeptic, or believer, his life and teachings offer profound insights into the nature of God, humanity, and the ultimate purpose of life.**

# ABOUT THE CREATOR

Walter the Educator is one of the pseudonyms for Walter Anderson. Formally educated in Chemistry, Business, and Education, he is an educator, an author, a diverse entrepreneur, and he is the son of a disabled war veteran. "Walter the Educator" shares his time between educating and creating. He holds interests and owns several creative projects that entertain, enlighten, enhance, and educate, hoping to inspire and motivate you. Follow, find new works, and stay up to date with Walter the Educator™

at WaltertheEducator.com

9 798330 450213